Where Will
We Live If the
House Burns
Down?

Previous Books by Allison Blevins

HYBRID
Cataloguing Pain

HYBRID CHAPBOOK
fiery poppies bruising their own throats

CREATIVE NONFICTION
Handbook for the Newly Disabled, A Lyric Memoir

POETRY
Slowly/Suddenly

POETRY CHAPBOOKS
Chorus for the Kill
Susurration
Letters to Joan
A Season for Speaking

Where Will
We Live If the
House Burns
Down?

Allison Blevins

A Karen & Michael Braziller Book
PERSEA BOOKS / NEW YORK

PERSEA BOOKS, INC.
90 Broad Street
New York, New York 10004

LIBRARY OF CONGRESS CATALOGING-IN-PUBLICATION DATA
Names: Blevins, Allison, 1980– author.
Title: Where will we live if the house burns down? / Allison Blevins.
Description: New York : Persea Books, 2024. | "A Karen & MichaelBraziller Book". |
    Summary: "Straddling genres, simultaneously real and surreal, Where Will We Live If
    the House Burns Down? explores the effects on a marriage of chronic illness, disability,
    and a spouse's gender transition. 2023 Lexi Rudnitsky Editor's Choice Award
    winner"—Provided by publisher.
Identifiers: LCCN 2024031250 (print) | LCCN 2024031251 (ebook) |
    ISBN 9780892555956 (paperback ; acid-free paper) | ISBN 9780892555970 (ebook)
Subjects: LCGFT: Prose poems.
Classification: LCC PS3602.L4755 W47 2024 (print) | LCC PS3602.L4755 (ebook) |
    DDC 811/.6—dc23/eng/20240708
LC record available at https://lccn.loc.gov/2024031250
LC ebook record available at https://lccn.loc.gov/2024031251

Book design and composition by Rita Skingle
Typeset in Arno Pro
Manufactured in the United States of America. Printed on acid-free paper.

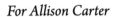

For Allison Carter

Under this mask another mask.
I will never finish removing all these faces.
    —CLAUDE CAHUN

In retaliation. In rhyme.
Among cherry blossoms blowing in wet, blowing snow,
weren't we something?
    —JAMES GALVIN

Where Will
We Live If the
House Burns
Down?

Grim often finds herself lost in the basin as if a void or whorling cosmos has opened in her bathroom. It's the water. How in rushing and rushing across her hands— how *rushing* isn't the right word but the sound of *rush* as in *gush* as in *sloosh*. How sound reverberates in both eardrums, and her legs feel drips and fire. She is gone. I can't say where. Her body remains. This loss lasts only seconds because there are the children. Always the children. Touching her legs and hair and arms.

The Sergeant won't eat ice cream from the pint after it's been opened, scooped, placed back in the freezer. Only untouched. Only smooth and unblemished. *Come on. We all think this is a metaphor.*

I patch Grim together like an exquisite corpse. Blinking eyes on her breasts and labia and knees. Grim is badly drawn. Grim is always blinking—sleepy. I can't compose the Sergeant. I try. I want. I fold and fold and fold. The page always white when I unfold and flatten the white against the table.

Some days Grim cannot peel herself from the bed. She is two dimensional—paper with sticky backing— sunflower wallpaper scraped to curls, creeping around the room in a breeze. She can't smile over risotto or green beans: *You can't know unless you've watched your life move on from the bed and wanted so hard to both walk to the table and to die at the same time.*

Medical waiting rooms remind Grim of breathing or eating—how we all do this strange moving together as marionettes. Like smelling armpits or ear wax or maybe dead skin squeezed from a tight black pore. Like remembering the weight of a past lover on your body. Like breaking apart or sewing together. Grim thinks of all the bears and cats and llamas she's re-seamed with thread. Think of your own intangible pieces that once gapped. For a child, this being sewn is alchemy. Like the beast come to life and roaring. Waiting together is like almost touching the tender slit between two toes—touch that is not yet touch. Medical waiting rooms always have an old man clearing his throat. This is standard. And his wife of forty-seven years hears the phlegm rattle his trachea. Again.

Grim tells the son he is swimming in a light she can't touch: *You never forget how your baby looked in your arms, in your body. I carry your swaying, your twitches and jerks always, inside my body.*

Another of Grim's cousins has been diagnosed with MS—four out of twenty-five on her mother's side. Her uncle said at the first of his siblings' funerals, *Eleven of us and not one divorce.* A younger Grim thought he made marriage seem like a job. All she can think about is dismemberment: *Here is a bit of skin, I've been saving this for you. Take both my aortas, plaque removed. Would you like my eyes? Left or right? We will never be strangers if you've swallowed a sliver of my fingernail.* Grim has eaten pieces of all her children: a bit of cuticle, a lick of salt from their eyes.

I'm worried Grim is becoming the central figure of this story. I didn't plan it. But here we are anyway. I should mention those nights—giddy on ecstasy—a lover brushed Grim's curls straight. How the comb trilled static against her back. Or how one of her lovers killed a friend with a car. Or how one burnt down a house in revenge. Thought it was empty. Or how one held Grim by the throat in a wet alley. In the grocery store when the son was a baby, he vomited as he played in the seat of the metal cart. Grim caught the vomit in her hands like they were a bowl. I think that may be what love looks like. We are not held but bound to each other. Eventually, there was nothing left to do but toss the vomit to the floor. No one came to save her.

Everything they need to know about war, they learn in bed together. The Sergeant makes Grim a damsel—red-hooded, eyes veering off the path—with thrusts and strikes. I watch her be stripped naked. Everyone is hungry. Everyone wants to eat. Make her a pedestal. The daughters—her daughters—I am the voice in their ears, the wolf long-low howling.

Grim thinks often about the king of the birds: *Churren,* the old man, and disease. Everywhere disease. Everywhere, the body wants to kill the body. Grim calls every king she sees blue withdrawal, their bird cry is heart-sick-bone-sick-nerve-sick—the sound greenpurple. Grim is wilting under the weight of so many fallen feathers. *No.* She is molting.

The daughter tells Grim she needs green gloves for swimming. Green to the elbow. The youngest wants a teacup covered in fur. Preferably fox. Head and tail attached. Grim sits with the family at dinner, *Today, the body feels okay. Not good. The body is golden and rounded at the corners, wishes to be square.* Some days, pain is so orderly it feels good as lined up shoes or boxcars in a tight row.

Grim can speak to the children. All three are the same as her. Like speaking to her hand or knee. Grim and the Sergeant grow cold each morning like oatmeal. Is this how we all are meant to feel? Will all someday feel? Congealed?

She writes letters to the children, silent in the head, every night to help her find sleep. Children are literal and also a device meant to evoke a feeling. I'm not sure what feeling. *Save the Children. Women and children first. See.* Now you feel something. Now you look to your own child—twelve and kicking a ball or four and grubby with chocolate, clutching a family quilt. Or you picture television children, nephews, or the girl from down the street out at night alone on her pink three-wheel bike. Everyone has a string to pull labeled *Child*. The son, the daughter, and the youngest eat pizza on a blue snowflake blanket some nights. The Sergeant writes a letter to the son every year on his birthday. Saves it in the closet for someday.

When a letter begins with *You*, I'm certain what comes next will be *Goodbye*. Grim can't stop imagining the Sergeant in bed with another person, entering them from behind or their bodies pushed tight together against a wall. Grim is certain this is punishment for becoming fat. She wants to remember fat sneaking up on her, but it wasn't like that. Fat was intentional: frosting from the can.

At the son's first funeral, he stands over the powdered body and asks, *Does the carcass take all that jewelry when it goes?* He has only read about the dead, only animals—mostly deer and dogs, a spider. This reading was intended to teach empathy. Grim tells him not to say *carcass*. The son laughs and laughs, holds Grim's hand tighter and tighter. They've discussed this laughing before. She puts her arm around his shoulders. Laughter is the same as sobbing from behind—all the cousins and uncles in the filling pews behind them. Laughter is the body pushing grief out from the shoulders in shudders.

Grim's pain doctor asks what her goals are. I want to tell him the chronically ill don't have goals. They don't want to be ill. Grim wants her old body back. She doesn't want to be in his office. Grim tells the doctor, *I want to stand long enough to make grilled cheese, want to walk the dark living room at night to check the children are breathing.* She wants to say absurdly large sunflowers block her path, her hair floats toward the ceiling as if her body is sinking in water, the flowers vine out and wrap her hips and arms like a handshake. She wants to stop the knife from cutting into her head like cooked meat on a platter of lettuce and tomatoes.

The Sergeant loves like a boulder, tumbling and crashing. Like a sea urchin spine stuck into a bare foot. The Sergeant never takes off the boots sewn into his ankles' delicate skin. Boots are preventative. Imagine his boots walking on piles of bones, how from a great distance this bleached white mass melts into mouths of *oh* and *ah* faces—masks of human faces like stretched and melted rubber, like taffy pulled and pulled. Grim and the Sergeant both like the chew and chemical tang of banana taffy. *Irrelevant.*

I carry their portraits with me—Grim, the Sergeant, the children. Watercolor on canvas. Grim asks to write letters to her surgeon—anesthesia and morphine stupor. She wants to know how many stitches. Grim and the Sergeant have a fight—they tight smile, angry whisper. Grim says she is writing a screenplay in her head. The Sergeant tells Grim she is speaking *gibberish*. The reel behind them glows. Grim substitutes objects for all of the characters. The son will be fingernail clippings. The daughter, a stuffed dog. The youngest, white petticoats. Gibberish. *Fine*, Grim whispers, *I'm calling my mother.* Nurses teach Grim how to get out of bed. In the screenplay, she is a felled tree. Grim has lost all feeling in her breasts and the fat pockets under her arms. I wonder if her audience wants to hear about each relapse in detail. In the mirror, Grim notices grimace lines around her mouth. She rocks the body as if cradling an infant. Here is where we edge too close to sentimental. Perhaps only the ill and broken notice how mourning is both being veiled and the veil lifting.

Grim wants to tell the Sergeant there is a dictionary for grief. But he wouldn't look up from his book. She fantasizes about thin pink wafers lined with pink cream and crisp-still-warm meringues. Sugar melting on the tongue. I want to say this is how Grim tastes, but I don't mean to you. I mean to me. Packed in that crisp thick melting is the body. Grim wants to convince the Sergeant she is still inside her body. Make him a believer again. She pretends to still experience the nuance of touch—tickle, prick, tongue—but it is all just pressure. She moans anyway. The neurologist pricks her legs with a safety pin some visits, tosses the pin into the garbage pail when she leaves the exam room. Grim keeps a collection of all the pins in a secret drawer with her children's baby teeth in labeled plastic baggies.

Reminisce sticks to the ill how sunglasses violet-tint hands, like emerald-cut jewels in art deco settings. I want to change *nostalgia* to mean laughter without the undercurrent nipping at the red-welting corners.

Here—midwest and spring and finally, finally green—
wide swaths of fields press into Grim's throat. In field
after field, a Zimmatic's arched metal trusses swing
circles of green. Turbine arms crisscross shadows onto
the green. Scripture on homemade white billboards
and gravel roads plume like fire in the distance. Smoke
seems to push and push into her throat. I declare her
minivan the department of pain management. 55 mph
hummmmm, the sound Grim hears when doctor after
doctor tells her to do something new.

Grim sits in the car outside the pain clinic. A patient smokes and paces with a limp that matches Grim's. They smile at each other. When Grim's mother comes to the house to watch the children, the mother folds the laundry—always waiting—in the white plastic basket. She can't stop herself. She folds their underwear into neat tight squares. That is the love Grim wants from those responsible for her body. As I write, I wish I could insert authorial omniscience, proclaim *this* was the moment I realized what would happen.

Every room is a ticking clock. Only, the Sergeant doesn't see how sound reverberates in the children's chests. Grim can see how a hyena sips at the corners of their canvas. Grim knows a Sphinx—doll head, black shawl, and her hanging flayed heart—tightens her arms around their chests, hugs them all tighter and tighter in their crumbling house.

Grim remembers a fall day when she was girl. She sat sweatered on her parent's brown sectional sofa. Rain fell—not a drizzle or a deluge—just fell, midwestern rain in November. The house was warm, and she was warm in it. She remembers. This is how it feels to be whole and surrounded by soft. Years later, in Wisconsin winters, the lakes frozen and silenced—interrupted only by shifting and cracking—filled her ears like the moan of a caged moon and ground stars waiting for casing and boil.

On a car trip once, the Sergeant explained force. Grim's father gets more racist the older everyone gets. Perhaps he is just more honest now. So many car trips together. Neurologist, MRI, endocrinologist, psychiatrist, spine surgeon, pain doctor, pharmacist. They argue about systemic racism. Grim's father couldn't tell who of her friends was a boy and who a girl on his first visit to see her at college. Once, Grim's father carried her adult body like a baby through a building screaming, *Help me!* Imagine polka dots. Dots swarm your eyes like a house of mirrors painted in mustard yellow. I once accidentally filled my palm with *Orange Goop* in a truck stop bathroom. Grim's memories are like that— rubbing and scrubbing and rinsing and a firmly, never-leaving layer—be careful where you put your hands.

Grim finds herself lost in her face reflected in the metal toaster. Slats shrink her head, point her nose. She is lost as if circling an endless well. She eats four frozen waffles every day. Real butter. No syrup. We might imagine the Sergeant has concerns. Primarily, how to stack all the boxes in the deep freeze. Every day, Grim's hair grays more and coils untamed into the air. She drinks only water from cans—carbonated, flavored with chemicals. *Did you think she was the heroine? Well. Maybe she is. You haven't read the ending yet.* For now, I mention this to show flaws. We might call her character developed. Grim thinks drinking water from cans is a mostly female activity. Before, she didn't think much about which activities were female, except in her classrooms. Except as theory. As a lesbian, she didn't concern herself much with men. Then the Sergeant was a man. Then the son was ten. She thought she could carry time—a twin bell analog clock—in her handbag of troubles. Then the son was eleven. Then twelve. *I understand this is how aging works.* I suspect Grim never thought the son would one day become a man. She imagined she could carry him in her green cloak forever. His green eyes a mirror of her green eyes. His body part of her body. He would live in her cloak folds forever.

The Sergeant and Grim warm some nights. They come together in their bed. But he is behind her, never looks at her face. The Sergeant asked Grim to take antidepressants. This was months ago, but she thinks about it often. She takes them. She agreed the Sergeant was right. He asks her to take more and she does. I'm tempted to make the Sergeant the villain, but I also hope you don't see him like that.

Grim sits on the sofa, sits on the bed. Green robe and tatty nightgown. Socks pulled up to knees keep her ice legs warm. Grim imagines socks keep the condensation dripping from her legs from ruining the floors, socks like cotton coasters. She knows her daughters see her stomach and face and arms swelling and swelling from ice cream and bread and crackers. She tells herself every night, *Tomorrow will be better.* Tomorrow, she won't eat sugar or gluten or dairy. She grows each night, wakes to find her pants too tight and shirts too short on her belly. Grim thinks she can starve herself, wishes people could see her toes seize or her foot turn sharply upwards as her calf squeezes and squeezes. Clearly, I want you to understand it too. My right finger twitches into the air sometimes when I type, comes down hard accidentally on *h* or *y* or *j*.

I used to be sharp. Now I am shattered. I email my writing partner to ask: *What's the thing that goes under cups on tables?* How must the Sergeant see Grim now? I want to write that their love blooms from wounds, from their cracks opened to red blood air. I want to say bodies, lined with silver are filling filling filling. The bodies might fill with water or birds or color—even my imagining is trite, repetitive. This is how we know what is really happening.

Videos of cysts pressed to popping. Singing competitions on television—but only the auditions where nearly everyone is winning and all the mothers sob from pride. Scones. Grim loves these things. Coffee too. Coffee with no sweetener. Coffee with half and half. Grim hates when semis make left turns in front of her at four-way stops and she is stopped first in the turning lane. They get closer and closer and closer. She hates her ex-wife. She once asked her father if he *knew a guy*. She wants to hate the Sergeant's ex-wife. But Grim imagines they might have much to say to each other. When the Sergeant lived on Ohio Street with the first wife, police found a man in a deep freeze in a house on Vermont Street. His wife had kept him there for six years. No foul play was discovered. I think this says something about the nature of wives. The Sergeant is still bothered such a thing could happen so close, only a few letters between him and the finality of a freezer. I can't tell you what the Sergeant loves or hates. At night he sits in the living room. Grim is on the bed.

Grim has intimate friends. Emotional cheating. We'd all call this *irony* even though it isn't. Grim's intimacies started after.

If you aren't ready to know what is true, you should never look at messages on your spouse's phone.

Grim is lucky to exist only on the page. Grim is not obligated to adhere or behave. Here is where and when to speculate, to say *I imagine*. Say it once out loud. I say it now to remind you we all have flaws.

The Sergeant imagines his body as a landscape—center mass is an island, tropical, and water water water. Water reflects the stars reflecting light and everything is glowing—second star from the right and so very far from home. I realize now the Sergeant has a story you won't find on these pages. *Growth*, Grim's therapist might say.

The pharmaceutical company calls occasionally to check on Grim. They want to make sure she keeps taking their medicine. They are emotionally supportive. It annoys her. On one call, the nurse tells Grim she can drink alcohol on the medication as long as it isn't near the time she takes the medication. We must call this *irony* as well. *I know, I know.* Grim tells her friend Meret one of the side effects of the medication is severe abdominal cramping. Grim says, *Like early labor.*

Everyone tells Grim she looks great, beautiful. *Aren't we all beautiful? This isn't helpful.* She wants to know what it feels like to watch someone you love disintegrate. *Tell me how it feels.* Grim is dying. *Aren't we all?* That isn't helpful. Grim is dying faster. Grim is a character played by the woman she once was. Grim draws on eye bags with makeup, paints her face flushing red. Grim collects her walker from the stagehand and foot drops her way on stage right.

Meret tells me the action of creating watchers and their perceptions will always be fiction. *What must be true or might be true?* Meret says it is beautiful how *must* means *maybe.* I tell her Grim wants to understand. *Don't sugarcoat it. Everyone does.* Grim wants someone to tell her she looks like shit. Meret suggests I ask Grim's parents or children. *Mom. Dad. How does it look to watch your child sick with a progressive neurological disease? How does it feel?*

Grim is obsessed with reading all of her clinical notes. She knows many of her doctors must dislike her. Hate her. Grim is described as *pleasant*. Pleasant! How this annoys her.

In the car after a trip, they argue. The one they have on repeat like some distant moon's orbit, like laundry, like the children's running path around the kitchen island. Grim asks the Sergeant what he needs. *I need you to need less from me.*

Grim's needs could fill a bucket—water drained from clogged pipes—and tie to the Sergeant's neck with a sharp tensile string. *Aren't people meant to grow and change?* I won't let Grim say she wants the Sergeant as the man he is now and she wants the woman he was before too. This isn't totally true. Shifts in the plates sent cracks streaming in diagonal rivers from their doorway molding before. The marriage has always been shifting. Isn't that how it goes? *Isn't that how it is meant to be?* Grim can't say a softness, a kindness has gone from his words and the pressure of his fingers, once gentle on her back as they walked through a crowded room, now absent. Grim can't say when all her losses happened.

Grim's therapist tells her she can't ignore the Sergeant's transition. *I'm not ignoring it. I just don't care.* The therapist *tsk-tsk's* tongue against teeth. No one believes Grim when she says there isn't enough room for all of the moving pieces. It's impossible to pull one bolt or crank handle from the clanging machinery. I know this paragraph will ruin them both. I shouldn't have written it. Everyone wants Grim to talk, to say how different he is now. Some of you want it too. Grim cries in the car. The Sergeant doesn't touch her neck or clasp her hand. Instead, he explains how he never enjoyed sex before. *Don't you want me to be happy?* And she is. *Happy.* Happy is pouring down her face. All those nights they spent together falling in love were before. He asks if the vacation was good for her. *Yes, but.* The Sergeant says, *See. There is always a but. That is what I asked you not to do.* Grim has trouble following conversations. Fog has seeped in through her cracks. Grim asks him to speak slower, kinder. The Sergeant has the last word. *The fog,* he says, *is only going to get worse.*

When she is doing dishes alone in the quiet house, all Grim can think about are the text messages between the Sergeant and the ex-wife. That one where he made a joke about her walking. She doesn't care about them meeting, what happened when they looked at each other again, when their eyes met. Grim can't look at his face without thinking about his words. How casually some men dismiss words. I want to make Grim tell her therapist the day he sent that text was *the* day. That was the moment. But she isn't ready.

They must start again. Grim begs him over and over. Silence screams from her mouth. She begs the Sergeant to apologize again and again. Each time his mouth is only buzzing. The Sergeant used to guide Grim through crowds with his hand on the small of her back. Sweet and gentle pressure. Ownership. *This belongs to me.* Grim loved it. She suspects the Sergeant no longer does this because he is terrified anyone could think such a gnarled and rusted thing belongs to him, as if he'd brought a bag of his garbage to the party.

Or is this just the middle?

The Sergeant packs on his underwear each morning. Grim sometimes watches his back from their bed, his face reflects in the mirror hanging behind the *his* of their his and hers vanity sinks. He never notices her watching and wanting. The Sergeant spends all of his free time in the bathroom peering into his mounted 10x magnification mirror. Grim bought the mirror as a gift. He wouldn't stop stealing hers. Grim's is only 5x. *That's love,* she thought at the time. That's love.

The son is so much Grim. When the two stand alongside each other and the sun from a near window runs between their bodies, mother and child bend light— light like snakes and clouds and cotton around and from their bodies. Grim remembers her eyes making shapes and sounds and monsters when she was young and on drugs. Before she was Grim—before she was mother or wife or body locked into a body—she was a girl so light she had to take drugs to tether her body to the ground. She had to cut neat rows into her arm and leg. The rows were to remind her then that she even lived in a body. Next to her son, Grim can feel his weightless body searching for an anchor. Before he was a son or child, he was the air she coughed from her black slicked nose and lungs, the blood she wiped from rows into her skin to pink, to paint patterns, the blood she licked from her salted fingers.

Before the Sergeant was the Sergeant, he was dandelion milk, green and tacked to his mother's fingers. He was a dish of cream and berries. He was a roller skate, a ponytail, a piano, a field of cows, wild yowling barn cats.

Like birches, the daughter guards the house, makes her arms into gears and pulleys. She is of use. Like car-lined residential streets. Like book-lined shelves. Like coat-lined closets. Wallpaper. Pedestrians. Rugs. Grease. Leaves. The daughter wraps them all in her long golden blanket, squared with black and green patchwork like a kiss. The daughter remembers every number, knows how to tie a bandage. One day, the daughter will tell her children about her singing. Like calming echoes—the tweets and trills of everyone who ever left—like picks buried hilt deep in rock, her canary voice skims around every room in the house.

Some nights, Grim and the Sergeant sit together in silence on the bed. *Companionable.* The large orange cat between them snores low and deep. An inexperienced observer of sleeping cats might imagine the snore begins in the bulge of belly. The cat often attacks segments of legs unexpectedly while the Sergeant pushes ground meat in a pan or shaves. Only the Sergeant and the daughter. The daughter is an antagonist cat lover. The daughter can't let sleeping cats sleep. She must press her face into the soft tufts of fur between ears like Grim presses her face into the bottom of her children's feet, smells the soft crevice where toes bend—this is the smell that binds mother to child.

Grim's mother tells the story over and over, as mothers past 70 often do. The mother has so many more stories about Grim's brother. Grim finds it difficult to feel pleased, but at least there is a story of her at all. The story claims Grim wanted to be a ballerina or brain surgeon. Grim believes this story is true only for her mother. The story is made true only in the telling and retelling. The mother loves the grandchildren. She calls them 1, 2, and 3 to make things easier.

I want Grim to tell the children about that bridge over the Mississippi. On the Missouri side, machines harvest and bale cotton. Cotton drifts snow-ward, sticks in the deep green roadside grass. And a dust haze fogs the highway air and throats.

As a child, Grim waited alone inside the car once a week while the mother shopped for groceries. She wrote screenplay treatments in her head about young girls abandoned by their mothers in cars outside small Kansas grocery stores. One movie girl spends most of the movie researching how to pay a mortgage absent a grown-up. From a car window, a child might mistake the glint of sun off car roofs as waves and crests. This is how Grim learned the magic of motion. Like how—as a child—your feet and thighs still roll in figure eights as you lace your sneakers and walk to the car after roller skating.

Before the Sergeant was the Sergeant . . . I want to tell Grim she has to think more intently about this. She must, but she folds him into a neat square and puts him in her pocket.

Evenings, Grim sits on the sofa with ice on her face and back after a shower transforms her to red and tight-chest burning. The daughter hovers, offers to bring more ice. On days when rain floods down their street, the daughter texts Grim to remind her of the umbrella in the glovebox. Grim never uses an umbrella. When offered an umbrella, she always says, *No. Thank you. I lived in Oregon in my 20s.* Most people respond, *Hmmm.* Her answer is nonsensical. Grim gives it anyway. She remembers the mountains, remembers the thin everyday film of water on her eyelashes and brows, how every deck was always green and moss slicked.

I imagine most people masturbate when they have the house alone for over an hour—especially married folks and the elderly, the most lonely. Grim has internalized hatred of the aging body. If this is just the middle, if they can just keep going. Where will we live if the house burns down?

At bedtime, the youngest finally puckers her baby-fat lips, pulls up half of Grandma Verla's old quilt and the corner of a pink plush blanket bought new, and rolls onto her right side. She settles into the mattress like I've seen dogs do. She will be asleep by the time Grim reaches her bedroom. This is the routine that lasts hours—milk, water, snacks, diapers, books, BAND-AIDS, more books. This is the joy I tried to explain to an old friend as we wrote together one weekend. *Ensconced.* Mostly the friend and I listened to each other and agreed—*you're so right*—the game women need to play with each other to feel alive. Grim feels this joy in her hips. Joy radiates down her left leg from her sacrum to the top of her foot. Joy thickens in the long muscles in the backs of her legs, wraps itself like a glove might each finger around her chest and hugs and hugs and hugs. Joy settles on her like dirt on pavement after a pelting winter rain.

Before the Sergeant was the Sergeant, he was a beggar star forcing his hands in car windows. His holy sighs like a sign: *The End is Near*. Pink and green and yellow—like chalk transferred to pants from a child's driveway portraits. He forced his arms and feet into his house, his bedroom, even his own mouth.

Some nights, Grim folds her body over the body of the sleeping son in his bed like origami, thinks of all the mothers who have made their bodies into this shape as bombs drop, guns click their self-righteous click before bang—men go about their violence.

Now it is July outside. Grim feels sorry for herself in a chair watching the impending dark. It smells like July and freshly-cut grass. The house windows—small squares like teeth. Grim wants someone who loves her to say, *Enough now. Too much.* But for the body in pain, every moment is an accounting of pain.

Wait. The Sergeant likes "Don't Stop Believin'" by Journey. Grim should know more than that by now. They fight often about *tone* and *intention.* These are code words for *I needed you to love me in that moment but you didn't.*

Grim told the Sergeant years ago that no relationship will work for her. Her brain is *divergent*. The son is divergent too. In both cases, *divergent* is code for *I speak literally. I understand literally.* Most people don't realize the world is not literal. The world is a scarecrow, head covered in a hat made of bees. The world is a child holding a small yellow ball of string. The world asks us to fling off our stockings, unwrap the wrappings that cling and cloak and whisp, grow antlers and flower the skin.

The world tells me the ending is always a woman's face cubed and squared. Don't try to move her pieces into a more pleasurable position. I painted the blue shoes, the bird belt, and the checkerboard pathway. Grab your umbrella in case I decide on rain.

Notes

This book would not have been possible without the work of Beth Ann Fennelly, Jenny Offill, Claudia Rankine, Prageeta Sharma, Sarah Manguso, Maggie Nelson, and Bhanu Kapil Rider.

Bridget Quinn's *Broad Strokes: 15 Women Who Made Art and Made History (in That Order)* and Whitney Chadwick's *Women Artists and the Surrealist Movement* heavily influenced my obsession with female artists and ekphrasis.

[Some days Grim cannot peel]: This section contains an allusion to Charlotte Perkins Gilman's "The Yellow Wallpaper."

[Grim thinks often about the king]: This section references Flannery O'Connor's "The King of the Birds."

[The daughter tells Grim she needs]: This section references Meret Oppenheim's *Objet.*

[Grim's pain doctor asks]: This section references Dorothea Tanning's *Eine Kleine Nachtmusik* and Julie Curtiss' *Food for Thought.*

[every room is a ticking clock]: This section references Leonora Carrington's *Self-Portrait* 1937–38 and Léonor Fini's *Petit Sphinx Hermite.*

[Grim remembers a fall day]: This section references Remedios Varo's *Papilla Estelar.*

[On a car trip once, the Sergeant]: This section references Yayoi Kusama's *Infinity Rooms.*

[Grim finds herself lost in her face]: This section references Remedios Varo's *Woman Leaving the Psychoanalyst.*

[The Sergeant imagines his body]: This section references *Peter Pan.*

Acknowledgments

Many thanks to the editors of the following magazines for publishing several of the pieces included here, often in earlier forms:

Brevity: A Journal of Concise Literary Nonfiction
Ghost City Press
Raleigh Review
Rust & Moth
The Night Heron Barks

Sections from this collection were selected as:
Honorable Mention for *Gulf Coast*'s 2023 Poetry Prize by judge Carmen Giménez
Finalist for the 2023 *Ninth Letter* Literary Awards
Finalist for the 2023 Geri Digiorno Prize from *Raleigh Review*

This book is dedicated to my dear friend Allison Carter. You are my fashion guru. Thank you for always telling me we will get through it together.

I owe much to the strong women in my life who have given selflessly and helped me keep moving through the muck. Thank you Laura Lee Washburn. For everything. Thank you Joan Kwon Glass for your humor and compassion. Thank you Michelle Hendrixson Miller for your care and generosity. Thank you Kristiane Weeks-Rogers for your support and organization. Thank you Julie Ramon and Dustin Brookshire for checking on me. To my mother and daughters, thank you for your beauty and love.

I am sincerely grateful for the help and encouragement of many writers and editors:

I'm incredibly lucky to have worked with the faculty at Queens. Thank you Sally Keith, Claudia Rankine, Morri Creech, Alan Michael Parker, and Jon Pineda.

Thank you Lynn Melnick for reading this manuscript and supporting my work.

Josh Davis, you are an incredible writing partner and friend. Thank you for loving me.

Thank you to the amazing staff at *Literary Mama* and *the museum of americana,* and thank you to everyone at MTSU Write for your support.

Thank you to my Small Harbor family. To all the staff and authors, I've been so lucky to work with all of you. Thank you Greg Stapp.

Kory Wells, Amy Cates, and Molly Jo Mullen, thank you for reading and critiquing several of the sections of this book, and thank you for the all the laughs.

Thank you to Ron Mohring, Danny Rosen, ME Silverman, Ami Kaye, Freddy La Force, Geoffrey Gatza, and KMA Sullivan for believing in my work and giving my books a home.

Justin and Alex Hargett at Kickflip Publicity, thank you for your dedication to this project.

Much of this book was written with the support of the Fayetteville Public Library while I was a Visiting Artist in the summer of 2022. Thank you to the staff and donors who made my residency possible.

Thank you Gabriel Fried and all the folks at Persea Books. This opportunity has been a dream come true. I'm grateful for the care and attention you've given this strange little book.

Taylor, you are, as always, the ground where I land and the air holding me together.

About the Lexi Rudnitsky Editors' Choice Award

The Lexi Rudnitsky Editor's Choice Award is given annually to a poetry collection by a writer who has published at least once previous book of poems. Along with the Lexi Rudnitsky First Book Prize in Poetry, it is a collaboration of Persea Books and the Lexi Rudnitsky Poetry Project. Entry guidelines for both awards are available on Persea's website (www.perseabooks.com).

Lexi Rudnitsky (1972–2005) grew up outside of Boston, and studied at Brown University and Columbia University. Her own poems exhibit both a playful love of language and a fierce conscience. Her writing appeared in *The Antioch Review, Columbia: A Journal of Literature and Art, The Nation, The New Yorker, The Paris Review, Pequod*, and *The Western Humanities Review*. In 2004, she won the Milton Kessler Memorial Prize for Poetry from *Harpur Palate*.

Lexi died suddenly in 2005, just months after the birth of her first child and the acceptance for publication of her first book of poems, *A Doorless Knocking into Night* (MidList Press, 2006). The Lexi Rudnitsky book prizes were created to memorialize her by promoting the type of poet and poetry in which she so spiritedly believed.

Previous winners of the Lexi Rudnitsky Editors' Choice Award